Frank Moriarty

MetroBooks

MetroBooks

An Imprint of Friedman/Fairfax Publishers

©2000 by Friedman/Fairfax Publishers

Library of Congress Cataloging-in-Publication Data available upon request

ISBN 1-58663-048-2

Editor: Nathaniel Marunas
Art Director: Kevin Ullrich
Designer: Jonathan Gaines
Photography Editor: Sarah Storey
Production Manager: Maria Gonzalez

Color Separations by Radstock Repro
Printed in England by Butler & Tanner Ltd.

10 9 8 7 6 5 4 3 2 1

For bulk purchases and special sales,
   please contact:
Friedman/Fairfax Publishers
Attention: Sales Department
15 West 26th Street
New York, NY 10010
212/685-6610 FAX 212/685-1307

Visit our website:
http://www.metrobooks.com

Contents

Introduction 6

Chapter One
A FAMILY'S
FOUNDATION 12

Chapter Two
FOLLOWING FOOTSTEPS . . . 20

Chapter Three
OPPORTUNITY KNOCKS 30

Chapter Four
WORKING FOR THE COACH . . 38

Chapter Five
TROUBLES AND TRIUMPH . . 48

Chapter Six
THE QUEST
FOR A CHAMPIONSHIP 60

Chapter Seven
DJ2K 82

Bibliography 94

Index 96

INTRODUCTION

Picture NASCAR, which is riding a stunning wave of popularity, at the dawn of the year 2000.... After years of letting individual racetracks make their own television deals, NASCAR and its sharp marketing people have stepped in and negotiated a massive multibillion-dollar broadcasting package that will move the sport onto the airwaves of major networks, ending the days of dependence on cable television outlets. Broadcasters like Pat Summerall, star anchor of the Fox network's NFL coverage, openly speculate that they may try their hand at covering stock car racing.

Longtime members of the motorsports media express outrage when a new policy is announced by NASCAR, whereby the sanctioning body will maintain full copyright

control over "the images, sounds and data arising from or during any NASCAR event." Once NASCAR courted any publicity; now it demands control over all images and how they will be used.

Legendary NASCAR car owners like Bud Moore, Junie Donlavey, and Cale Yarborough struggle to keep their teams alive, begging for sponsors or giving up entirely and seeking new owners willing to buy their equipment.

In the wake of a bitter battle among the open-wheel ranks of Indycar racing, the once-glamorous, costly race teams have chosen sides and compete in two separate series before dwindling crowds. With their eyes on the path of the sports marketing dollar, many top participants from the two series smell potential success in stock car racing. A buzz runs through the NASCAR garage as the open-wheel contingent sets its sights on the Winston Cup Series. From drivers Scott Pruett and Robby Gordon to car owner Cal Wells to famed engine-building company Cosworth, a well-funded invasion from far beyond the Southern roots of NASCAR appears to be imminent.

But reigning over the Winston Cup Series as champion is a man who brings comfort to those

Left: Ned Jarrett used the wisdom gained during a championship career racing in NASCAR to become one of the most beloved commentators in the world of motorsports broadcasting.

Opposite: More than three decades after Ned won his NASCAR title, son Dale Jarrett would match the feat.

Pages 8-9: The two Ford Thunderbirds of Robert Yates Racing, seen here in 1996 with Ernie Irvan at the wheel of the 28 and Dale Jarrett in the 88.

made uneasy by the dizzying pace of change. His pedigree is impeccable, his roots immovably intertwined with the history of stock car racing. His name is Dale Jarrett.

Now picture NASCAR decades before, when the millennium seemed a long way off and NASCAR tracks were just as likely to be dirt as asphalt. Today's million-dollar palaces of speed, with their corporate boxes and restaurants, are implausible dreams, and the men who pilot the stock cars are a rough-and-tumble bunch whose egos probably wouldn't swell even if they knew they were writing the racing legends of the future.

At many of the races, in the infields of the tracks, the families of the drivers can be found. The kids are just kids, even if their last names are Petty and Pearson. Among those youngsters is Dale Jarrett, the son of NASCAR champion Ned Jarrett. Whereas many drivers are known for wild behavior and almost unbelievable shenanigans, Dale's father is known as "Gentleman Ned." And the values that are associated with the word "gentleman" are passed on to Dale Jarrett and will come to imbue his own racing career.

Now, with the future of stock car racing in marketing-driven turmoil, longtime race fans see Dale Jarrett's ascension to the championship as a blessing—and as an important link to the history of a sport undergoing fundamental change.

This is the story of Dale Jarrett and his rise to the pinnacle of the Winston Cup Series.

Right: Dale Jarrett was raised in the world of NASCAR, but simply growing up playing with the children of other drivers is no guarantee of racing success—Dale has earned his victories by being a smart, courageous driver.

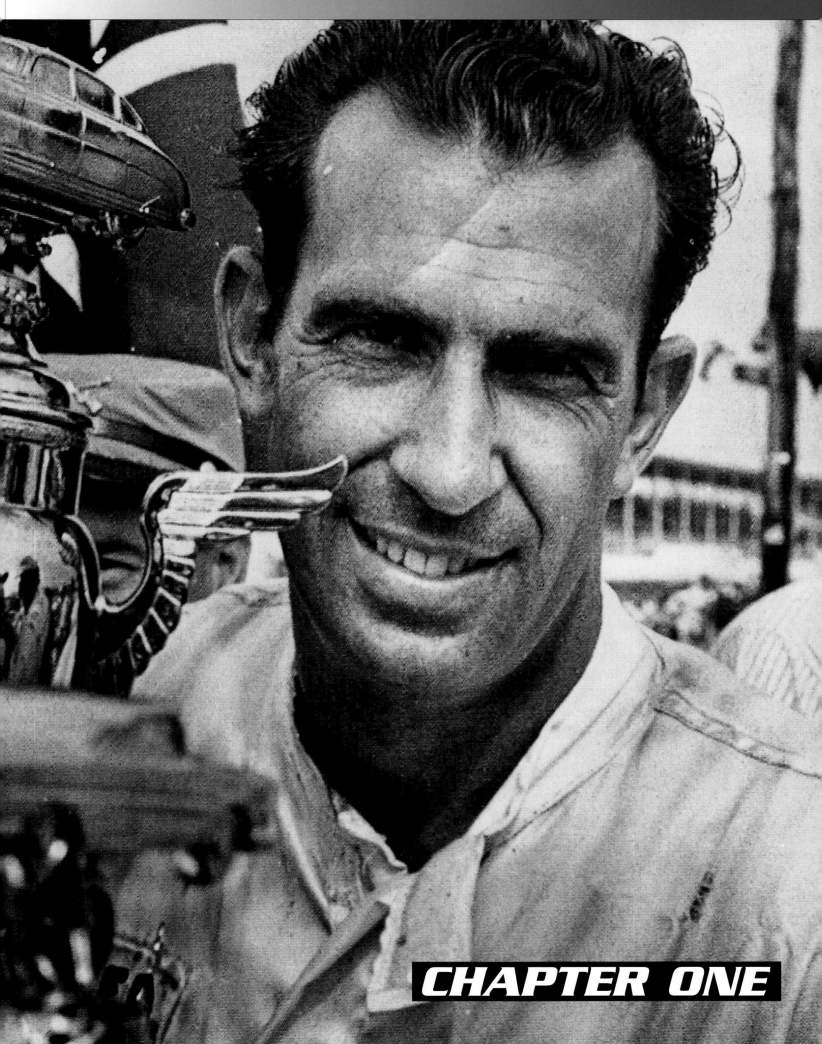

CHAPTER ONE

In 1953, a young man from North Carolina made his first start in NASCAR's Grand National Division. Though he finished well outside of the top ten, Ned Jarrett had begun a career that would have a lasting impact on the records of the National Association for Stock Car Automobile Racing, or NASCAR.

Ned Jarrett was born on October 12, 1932; his family was involved in farming and also ran a sawmill near the town of Conover. Ned had learned to drive trucks on the family farm well before his tenth birthday, and he had shown an early love for machinery. But young Ned's interest turned as a teenager to the construction of a new racetrack, the now-legendary Hickory Speedway. He began to see a way to combine his love of mechanics and his urge to compete.

Jarrett's father had taken him to races in the formative years of stock car racing, and the construction of the new dirt-surfaced track was quite an event in the rural area where young Ned lived. His interest was piqued in racing—but how to make the dream a reality?

When a rainy day found Jarrett, a friend named David Lentz, and others in a poker game, a winning play led to Jarrett and Lentz walking away as co-owners of a $200 race car. In the first race held at Hickory Speedway, Jarrett finished tenth and from that point on he never looked back.

But as is often the case in racing, this driver's family was less than thrilled about his motorsports activities. So Ned handed the driving chores over to Lentz—until one night when Lentz was sidelined by illness.

Jarrett filled in behind the wheel, masquerading as his sick partner and taking the car to a second-place finish. From then on Jarrett manned the

Pages 12-13: Victory in the fabled Southern 500 is a highlight of any driver's career, and that was even truer in the early days of the Grand National Series. Here Ned Jarrett savors his prestigious victory at Darlington in 1965.

Right: Today's fans, accustomed to seeing drivers wearing closed-face helmets equipped with air recirculators, may be surprised at the no-frills safety equipment worn by Ned Jarrett in this 1953 photograph.

Opposite: No matter how racing has changed over the decades, fire is still one of the sport's greatest dangers. Ned Jarrett escaped uninjured from this pit road conflagration in 1965.

driver's seat, at first continuing in the guise of Lentz, but eventually—and with his father's blessing—racing under his own name.

Success came to Jarrett in the sportsman racing classes, but he was drawn to NASCAR's top divisions. The sanctioning body was gaining a foothold in the South and building a foundation for national success, and Ned wanted to try his hand at the highest level of stock car competition. From 1953 until 1958, he made just a handful of starts and found little success. But he kept trying, showing the determination that has come to be associated with the racing Jarretts.

Above: Having changed brands from Chevrolet to Ford, Ned Jarrett powers through a turn in 1965, the year he drove to his second Grand National Series championship.

Opposite: Racing in North Carolina in 1961, Jarrett's Chevrolet carries the familiar number 11 that would identify him during his greatest years as a NASCAR competitor.

In 1959, in seventeen starts, Jarrett won twice. He was on his way. In 1960, he challenged NASCAR's best forty times and came away the winner in five of those contests. He was racing in stock cars much heavier than today's specially built Winston Cup vehicles, wrestling a car converted from a street automobile into a racer around everything from tiny dirt bullring racetracks to the huge superspeedway in Daytona Beach, Florida. And Jarrett was doing it against the most legendary names in stock car racing—drivers like Junior Johnson, Ralph Earnhardt, Richard Petty, and David Pearson.

The rivalry between Johnson and Jarrett was especially heated, to the point where NASCAR founder Bill France, Sr., felt the need to sit the two drivers down and defuse the growing feud.

In 1961, Jarrett won the Grand National championship, piloting his Chevrolet to one win and consistent top-five and top-ten finishes. His success caught the eye of Ford Motor Company's racing operations. Running for car owner Bondy Long, Jarrett won fourteen races in 1964. In 1965, he won his second championship while driving Long's Ford as part of a team of elite drivers, including Johnson, Glenn "Fireball" Roberts, and Marvin Panch, all aligned with the manufacturer. Jarrett could count on a (then-generous) paycheck of $2,000 for races of 250 miles (402.3km) or longer.

He won thirteen races and finished second the same number of times on his way to the title.

But the stock car racing world was stunned when, after the 1966 season, Jarrett retired from the driver's seat at the age of thirty-four. Ned had attained the goals he'd set out to achieve in NASCAR racing: to capture the championship and to win the fabled Southern 500 at Darlington Raceway, a victory he'd claimed on his way to his 1965 Grand National Series title.

Another factor in Jarrett's decision to retire was his concern for a stable source of income to support his family. He had seen fire claim the life of the legendary Fireball Roberts, and had witnessed the sometimes fickle actions of the manufacturers who battled with each other in NASCAR competition. Although racing had proven lucrative, perhaps a more dependable—and safer—livelihood was in order. After all, Ned and wife Martha had one son, Glenn, already in high school; not far behind was their youngest child, daughter Patti, as well as another son, ten-year-old Dale.

Though Ned Jarrett hung up his helmet, his strong-but-smart charges in races made a lasting impression not only on the sport of stock car racing, but on his youngest son as well.

Left: A proud father interviews his son, as Dale's quest to the 1999 Winston Cup championship rolls on. Despite his pride in his son's accomplishments, Ned is the consummate professional—his coverage of Dale has always been impartial.

CHAPTER TWO

Pages 20-21: *Contending for the Winston Cup championship was far in the future when this photograph, showing Dale Jarrett's crew in the process of diagnosing a problem at Martinsville Speedway in 1986, was taken.*

Left: *Almost every Winston Cup driver has started his career in circumstances like this. Here, Dale Jarrett (center) poses proudly in front of his car, ready for local short track competition in 1977.*

Opposite: *Dale Jarrett in 1986, the season that yielded his first Busch Grand National win. The next season, Dale entered full-schedule Winston Cup competition.*

Although Ned Jarrett had retired from racing, the sound of roaring engines still surrounded the family. Ned became manager of Hickory Speedway, the very track where he had first competed. But he was poised to make an even bigger contribution to the sport, one that would help expose millions of new fans to the action on the tracks of NASCAR.

In 1961, after winning his first championship, Jarrett was anxious to represent the sport well. At an Elks Club ceremony in North Carolina, he discovered, to his horror, that he could not remember a single word of a speech he was supposed to deliver. The next day, Jarrett (whose Grand National racing nickname was "Gentleman Ned," a moniker that perfectly described the man) called the number

in an advertisement for a Dale Carnegie course, determined to improve himself.

Using what he learned in the Carnegie course as the foundation for a post-competition career, Jarrett began to try his hand at radio broadcasting. It was a smart move, one that would eventually lead to his current position as the dean of television motorsports analysts.

But while Ned was establishing his path to the broadcast booth, his son Dale was already showing signs of following in his father's racing footsteps.

Born on November 26, 1956, Dale had grown up riding to races all across the South and playing in the racetrack infields with the children of other NASCAR competitors. His pals included Kyle Petty, the son of Richard; Davey Allison, the son of Bobby; and Larry Pearson, the son of David.

Not surprisingly, Dale showed the same interest in things mechanical that his father had shown during his own childhood. Like many children, Dale built model cars and played with go-carts, but unlike most kids, he grew up surrounded by real race cars.

Yet racing faced a serious challenge for Dale's affection as the youngster entered high school. Father Ned had taken a broken golf club, cut it down to his 12-year-old son's size, and watched as Dale took to the links with great enthusiasm.

Dale's passion for golf and his skill at the game increased rapidly as he entered Newton-Conover High School near the Jarrett family home in North Carolina. Though Dale played football, basketball, and baseball as he moved toward graduation, his

Above: Early in his career Dale Jarrett raced in the Goody's Dash Series, where the smaller "compact" cars go head to head on the big superspeedways as well as short tracks. Here, Jarrett's Busch car is ready to run at Charlotte Motor Speedway in 1980.

Opposite, top: Teams competing in the NASCAR levels below Winston Cup often have to deal with vehicles that are not as perfectly suited to racing as Winston Cup cars are. Here, one of Dale Jarrett's crew members hustles a heavy jack toward Dale's number 32 Budweiser ride in 1980.

Opposite, bottom: The sharp-angled stock cars of the 1980s, like this one driven by Dale Jarrett in 1984, were a far cry from today's more rounded racers, which emphasize aerodynamics.

But the peaceful concentration of the golf course had not completely pulled young Dale away from the noise and heat of the world of racing. In fact, after graduation, Dale worked at Hickory Speedway, the small but historic racetrack that his father managed. And though Dale continued to play golf, his choice of career became clearer in 1978.

That was the year when, teamed up with a young friend named Andy Petree, Dale became involved in a "project." The goal was to compete in the Limited Sportsman Division at Hickory. The weapon of choice was a 1968 Chevrolet Nova. Like Jarrett, Petree, as a crew chief and car owner, would go on to great success in Winston Cup racing. But for both men, that success was still a long way off.

record on the links was his most impressive athletic achievement. He led the Newton-Conover High School golf team to three championships in their conference. And he was named the school's athlete of the year as a senior in 1975.

In his first professional race, Dale Jarrett started twenty-fourth out of thirty cars at Hickory. When the checkered flag waved, Dale had raced to ninth place—and racing itself had beat out golf in Jarrett's heart.

"I knew after I drove that race that I wanted to race for a living," Dale later recalled. "I had become a scratch golfer and had thought seriously about trying to make a career of golf. I received a lot of encouragement from my parents about golf. Dad knew the hardships and pitfalls of racing and he didn't want me to go through them. My mother had

worried about Dad racing for years and she didn't want another one in the family to worry over.

"But there was no doubt in my mind about what I wanted to do. After Dad saw that I was serious about racing, he gave me his full support, as he would have done regardless of what I had chosen to do."

Unlike Dale's young playmates who had also decided on careers in racing, Dale was at somewhat of a disadvantage. When Davey Allison and Kyle Petty entered racing as a career, both of their fathers were still active and highly successful in the

Winston Cup Series. But Ned Jarrett had retired from Grand National racing almost a decade earlier. There were no hand-me-down race cars in the family for Dale to cut his competitive teeth on. Everything he got he had to earn.

Dale ran in the Limited Sportsman Division at Hickory in 1979, then moved to the subcompact cars of the NASCAR Dash Series in 1980. Then it was on to the Late Model Sportsman Division in 1981.

Opposite: The road to the Winston Cup Series is a long one. Like countless other drivers on the circuit today, Dale Jarrett cut his teeth in the Busch Grand National Series.

Below: Dale ran both his Busch Grand National car, seen here at Charlotte, and Freedlander's Winston Cup Chevrolet entry in competition during a busy 1987 season.

For 1982, NASCAR had plans to elevate the Late Model Sportsman Division into what has become today's Busch Grand National Series; Dale had plans to elevate himself right along with it. With a partnership formed along with his father and Horace Isenhower, Dale raced in twenty-nine events in the 1982 season, claiming top-ten finishes in more than half of the races and winding up sixth in points.

Though he consistently ran near the front of the pack in Busch Grand National competition throughout the 1980s—setting a pace that boasted more than fifty top-five finishes—the first win in this echelon of competition proved elusive. Finally, in 1986, at a tough short track just like those on which his father, had found success, Dale Jarrett drove to victory lane.

"It sure felt good to win," Dale remembered of the win at Orange Speedway in Rougemont, North Carolina. "I'd finished second at least a dozen times over the years."

But as important as it is to learn to win on the racetrack, it's equally important to know what must occur behind the scenes. "With just three people and limited sponsorship, we had to work long and hard," Dale said of his early career. "But that made me a better driver. I understand the building of a race car, what makes it go and how to set up one."

And though the Busch Grand National Series was taking up most of Dale's time in his new career, he had cast his eye toward NASCAR's elite Winston Cup Series.

Historic Martinsville Speedway, deep in Virginia, was the site of Dale's first foray into the top NASCAR series. In a Chevrolet owned by former Grand National winner Emanuel "Manny" Zervakis, Dale Jarrett found himself in combat with both the tight half-mile (0.8 km) speedway and NASCAR's greatest drivers. He battled his way from a twenty-fourth-place starting position to finish fourteenth, a most impressive run.

His sporadic Winston Cup starts and his strong runs in the Busch Grand National Series finally

Below: Dale Jarrett catches an eyeful of one of the most feared sights in NASCAR: Dale Earnhardt in the rear view mirror.

Opposite: On the track and in the garage, Jarrett learned valuable lessons while competing in the number 29 Pontiac for NASCAR legend Cale Yarborough in 1989.

began to pay off when Winston Cup team owner Eric Freedlander hired Dale five races into the 1987 season. Jarrett made the most of the opportunity, scoring his first top-tens in the top division. And while still running in the Grand National events, Dale won at the track that was so significant to the Jarrett family, Hickory Speedway.

When the year was over, Dale had run in fifty-one events in NASCAR's top two divisions.

In 1988, Dale ran again in both divisions. In the Winston Cup Series, he raced for both Hoss Ellington and the great Cale Yarborough. And his Grand National efforts paid off with a high-profile win at Charlotte Motor Speedway.

Cale Yarborough fielded Winston Cup cars for Jarrett in 1989, and Dale responded with several top-tens. But at the end of the season, Dale was released by Yarborough.

"It was a business matter," Dale explained. "Cale had lost his sponsor and couldn't commit to me. Then he got another sponsorship deal that involved another driver. That left me without wheels, but I have no hard feelings. Cale was able to keep his team together, and it would be a lot easier for me to find a job than for his whole crew if he had not struck a deal that didn't involve me."

As things turned out, Cale may have wished he had kept Dale Jarrett as his driver.

CHAPTER THREE

In February 1990, as the NASCAR Winston Cup Series arrived in Daytona for the annual season-opening Daytona 500, Dale Jarrett must have been disappointed. He'd become an established force in the Busch Grand National Series and had shown in his Winston Cup starts that he could race against the big boys. But as final preparations were being made for the biggest NASCAR race of them all, Dale was coping with having been released by Cale Yarborough from the team's Winston Cup ride. It seemed the aspiring young driver had no choice but to return to the Grand National Series.

But in early April 1991, Dale was presented with an opportunity that was almost beyond his wildest dreams. Neil Bonnett was one of the

Winston Cup Series' greatest drivers, a fan favorite, a close friend of Dale Earnhardt, and a member of the latest edition of the "Alabama Gang," the group of Southern racers based around Bobby and Donnie Allison. But racing for the Wood Brothers in the five-hundred-mile (804.5km) spring race at Darlington Raceway in South Carolina, Bonnett was involved in a terrible accident. Though he began to physically recover, he suffered from amnesia as a result of the violent impact he suffered at the wheel of his Thunderbird.

Soon after Bonnett's crash at Darlington, Dale Jarrett received a call from Eddie Wood. Wood was one of Jarrett's infield playmates from his youth and had now moved into a position of responsibility with the Wood Brothers racing team, one of

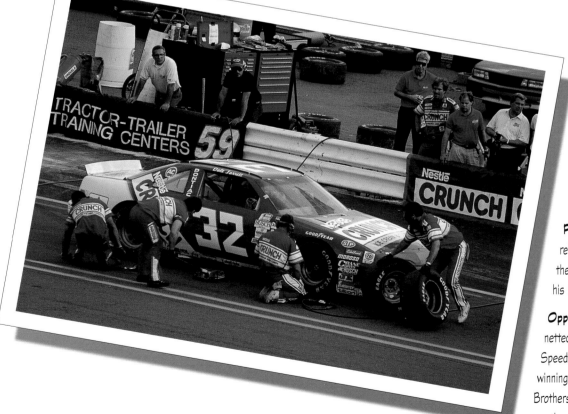

Pages 30-31 and left: Having been released from Cale Yarborough's team after the 1989 season, Jarrett began 1990 in his number 32 Busch Grand National car.

Opposite: Performances like the one that netted Dale this trophy at Charlotte Motor Speedway in 1990–part of a Busch Series-winning run–are what convinced the Wood Brothers Winston Cup team that Dale Jarrett was the driver to put in their car.

NASCAR's most famous teams. Would Dale like to fill in during Bonnett's recovery? Jarrett leapt at the chance.

"I'll be available to the Woods as long as they need me," Dale said at the time. "My first thoughts are with Neil and that he will be back soon. It's a tremendous opportunity in my situation to show what I can do in a real good car for a good team."

Below: Dale Jarrett in the 21 car thunders along on the first lap at Pocono International Raceway in June 1990. Just ahead of Dale runs Kyle Petty, who in turn, chases Alan Kulwicki.

"I'm not going to take foolish chances to get the car up front, but I'm going to race hard and be aggressive. That's how Neil drove it."

Sadly, though, Bonnett would never return to the Wood Brothers car. His recovery took many months, and when he was finally ready to return to the Winston Cup Series full-time in 1993, he was killed in a crash while practicing for the Daytona 500.

Dale Jarrett was right—this was his chance to drive "a real good car for a good team."

Founded by brothers Leonard and Glen Wood, the team had an impressive record that stretched

back to NASCAR's earliest days. Only the Petty family cars had attained a level of success to match that of the Wood Brothers. As the 1990 season dawned, their cars had won a total of ninety-four Winston Cup races, and their masterful preparations for superspeedway races accounted for seventy-eight of those wins. They had claimed more than 100 poles, and the list of Wood Brothers drivers who had preceded Dale Jarrett reads like a Who's Who of motorsports: A.J. Foyt, Bobby Rahal, Parnelli Jones, Curtis Turner, Junior Johnson, Buddy Baker, Fred Lorenznen, Dan Gurney, David Pearson, Donnie Allison, and many, many more.

If Dale was intimidated by the big shoes he had to fill, he didn't show it. After all, the Woods had recently had success with another of his childhood friends, Kyle Petty.

Dale's first run for the Wood Brothers came at one of NASCAR's toughest, most demanding racetracks. But in the five-hundred-lap event at Tennessee's Bristol International Raceway, Jarrett ran a gritty race and came away in eleventh place. Through the rest of the season, Dale managed seven top-ten finishes, his best being a fourth in Atlanta at the season's final race.

The 1990 season had been a season of getting acquainted with how to work with the Wood Brothers team, as team chemistry is crucial to success in Winston Cup racing. But now that precedents had been set, it was time to run for wins.

"I think you can only be as aggressive as the race car allows," Dale had said upon landing the Wood Brothers ride. "I never thought it was very intelligent to be running eighteenth and be aggres-

sive. You make a lot of people mad that way. There's no use to do stupid things to tear up a race car. Give me a front running car, though, and see how aggressive I am."

On August 18, 1991, Dale Jarrett had just such a car at Michigan International Speedway.

Leading up to the second Michigan race of the season, Jarrett had begun the year with a sixth in the Daytona 500, and he clawed closer to victory lane with a fifth in the season's longest race, the six-hundred-mile (965.4km) event at Charlotte Motor Speedway. But on-track conflicts had been plaguing many of the drivers in the Winston Cup Series. Before the race at Pennsylvania's Pocono International Raceway, Jarrett had had enough.

"There's been a blatant disregard and disrespect for other drivers lately, and I've been a victim," Jarrett fumed. "It looks like I'm going to have to quit worrying about whom I make mad or who I think my friends are."

Armed with his Wood Brothers Thunderbird and his new attitude, Jarrett qualified eleventh with a speed of more than 171 mph (275.1kph). And when the race began, he made it clear that his car was a contender. But it was late in the two-hundred-lap event when a thrilling drama began to play out.

The caution flag waved on lap 188, and the leaders dove toward their pit stalls. Mark Martin took on two tires and fuel, while Davey Allison, Ernie Irvan, Harry Gant, Rusty Wallace, Alan Kulwicki, and Bill Elliott all opted for four fresh tires. But the Wood Brothers made a bold call: take on fuel only.

When the race restarted, Jarrett had his work cut out for him. He was in front due to the swift work of his pit crew, but all of the top contenders behind him had new tires.

The restart was rough, but Jarrett managed to eke out a lead. Behind him, though, Davey Allison was on a mission. He rubbed his way past Mark Martin and set his sites on Jarrett's red-and-white Thunderbird. Allison's black Ford, powered by a strong Robert Yates engine, had been an intimidating presence all season, starting with victory in the Daytona 500. Daytona had been important, but Davey wanted this win, too.

Allison closed in on Jarrett's back bumper with fewer than five laps remaining. Then, as the flagman signaled two laps to go, Allison swung along the outside of Jarrett. The fans were on their feet. This was truly going to be a classic NASCAR battle to the finish.

Allison pulled slightly ahead as the white flag signaled the final lap, but Jarrett refused to give up. The two cars bumped going through the second turn, and bumped again and again through turns three and four, urgent clouds of white smoke issuing forth as the cars' tires rubbed at more than 170 mph (273.5kph). Toward the finish line, the Fords charged on, and no one knew what would happen.

Side-by-side the Thunderbirds roared across the finish line, and so close was the finish that it was up to the instant replays to offer proof that Dale Jarrett had just won his first Winston Cup race—by less than a foot (30.5cm). In the ESPN television booth high above the grandstands, father/commentator Ned Jarrett beamed proudly.

"You dream about winning races like that," a deliriously happy Dale Jarrett said. "Racing somebody like Davey Allison, to beat somebody like that at the end, to race him door-to-door."

The popular young driver was also thrilled to be able to pay back the Wood Brothers for their confidence in his abilities. After the race, a very happy Jarrett enthused, "When I crossed the finish line, I thought that I was ahead. I was just glad I was able to hold Davey off and make them the winners they are."

"I don't like second worth a flip," Davey Allison said to Dale in victory lane, "but if I have to finish second today, it's not too bad doing it to you."

Though Dale's victory was an ecstatic event, there was a bittersweet note to it. Days earlier, it had been announced that National Football League coach Joe Gibbs was starting a new NASCAR team. His driver for the 1992 season would be none other than Dale Jarrett.

Though he would be losing his driver at the end of 1991, Dale's friend Eddie Wood was able to put the Michigan race and Dale's first win in a happy perspective. Said Wood, "He got his first win in our car and we did it together. No one can ever take that away from us."

Opposite: Dale Jarrett finished this race at Pocono in June 1991 as the last car on the lead lap. Two months later, he reversed that order, winning for the Wood Brothers at Michigan.

CHAPTER FOUR

On August 13, 1991, the head coach of the National Football League's Washington Redskins, Joe Gibbs, held a press conference at the team training camp facility in Carlisle, Pennsylvania. The purpose: to announce that he was forming a NASCAR Winston Cup racing team.

NASCAR had been on a swift rise up from its moonshine-running roots to national legitimacy, and Gibbs' announcement was just the latest big step. Still, it was an important one. Here, one of the most visible figures in the world of "stick and ball" sports wasn't just showing an interest in stock car racing; he was becoming an active participant.

Gibbs explained to the assembled media that he had long been interested in all things automotive.

"When I was growing up in the fifties, it was cars and hamburger joints and I had just about every kind of street rod you could have," the coach warmly recalled. "It was a great time. We were having a ball, really, and I got into organized drag racing and had a tremendous interest in that area of competitiveness."

But Gibbs' involvement with football tore him away from the motorsports, much like Dale Jarrett had been forced to choose between golf and racing.

Pages 38-39: The Joe Gibbs racing pit crew springs into action at Charlotte Motor Speedway in 1992.

Below: Jarrett lifts the right front tire as he rockets around the Watkins Glen, New York, road course.

Opposite: Dale Jarrett had good reason to smile in 1992, as he had been picked to drive for a high-profile Winston Cup team. Joe Gibbs' decision to enter the world of stock car racing had attracted tremendous attention.

"You always have dreams," Gibbs said, "and mine was always… well, I had a fantasy of getting back into racing cars.

"Of course, I wanted to drive one. I think I've outlived that, but about two years ago I started seriously wondering if there was any way to get back into racing. There comes a time in life when you say, 'You can either grab a dream or let it slide by.' I grabbed it."

Gibbs had also grabbed Jarrett as his driver, and Jimmy Makar as his crew chief. It seemed a perfect pairing.

"When we started looking at people who would be interested in being part of our team," Gibbs explained, "I talked to drivers about drivers, crew chiefs about drivers, and to owners about drivers. I started doing research into who was available and, believe it or not, a lot of people were interested. It boiled down to where we felt Dale would fit in perfectly with us."

As for Makar, he had come into prominence as a chassis specialist with the Blue Max team and driver Rusty Wallace, helping to capture the 1989 Winston Cup championship. And when Rusty Wallace formed a new team with famed motorsports businessman Roger Penske and Don Miller, Makar was hired as the crew chief. To top things off, Makar was married to Dale Jarrett's sister, Patti.

With sponsorship lined up from Interstate Batteries and the decision made to run Chevrolet Luminas, Makar, Jarrett, and the newly assembled

Right: Two of NASCAR's newer stars battle side-by-side at Richmond International Raceway as Dale Jarrett, in the number 18 entry, holds off Jeff Gordon.

team faced a stiff challenge: build a winning operation from the ground up, and be ready to run in time for the 1992 Daytona 500.

In late December 1991, Dale Jarrett could be found trying out his new ride at a General Motors test session at Daytona International Speedway. With the season's biggest race

and his new team's debut just weeks away, Jarrett had a full agenda for testing.

"We have a number of things we test," Jarrett said while taking a brief break from the driver's seat. "Especially here at Daytona, there's so many different things. You have to cover all avenues because the speeds with restrictor plates have gotten so close that any little small gain you can make is a tremendous difference. We test anything from changing the body a little bit—maybe a little front fender change or in the cowl location—what's going to work best with that. Different gears, types of gears, rear end, ratchet, springs, shocks—there are many, many things. We've probably made thirty-five changes in the three days to see what's going to make the car go faster—and to eliminate the things that don't help."

When February rolled around, it was time to measure the fruits of the testing labors. But in racing, perhaps more so than in any other sport, the best-laid plans often go awry. Dale Jarrett was caught up in an accident during the race, and Gibbs saw his team's NASCAR debut go down in the history books as a thirty-sixth-place finish in the Daytona 500.

But soon enough there were signs of promise. The bright green car finished just outside the top ten at Atlanta in March, and April began with a runner-up showing at Tennessee's Bristol International Raceway, an intimidating track at which Dale Jarrett always seemed to perform well. And back at Daytona for the four-hundred-mile (643.6km) race in July, Dale raced to third place.

Above: Former NFL coach and new NASCAR team owner Joe Gibbs had to trust in the combination of the knowledge of his crew chief, Jimmy Makar, and the skills of his driver, Dale Jarrett. Gibbs had reason to have faith in the crew he had put together; his understanding of team dynamics had helped him build winning pro football teams in the past.

Opposite: The challenges of starting a new Winston Cup team are myriad, and the established teams are at a distinct advantage in terms of experience.

By season's end, the Joe Gibbs racing team and Dale Jarrett were often running in the top ten, a tremendous achievement for a brand-new team. And finishing nineteenth in the championship points wasn't bad, either. But Gibbs, Makar, and Jarrett wanted to be more than just contenders—they wanted to win.

On February 14, 1993, the green flag waved over the field of the Daytona 500 as a new season began. And as had so often been the case in previous years, Dale Earnhardt looked to be the class of the 500 field. The black number 3 Chevrolet led lap after lap, and after the race's final caution flag, due to a terrifying crash on the backstretch involving Rusty Wallace, Earnhardt had his sights set on finally breaking his Daytona 500 winless streak. But there was soon another Dale in the Daytona equation.

As the cars streaked across the finish line with two laps remaining, Earnhardt led Jeff Gordon and Dale Jarrett toward turn one. Jarrett knew his car was strong and that it would stick where he put it, so he made an uncharacteristic move in the thirty-one-degree banking of the first turn and swung high to the outside of Gordon's rainbow-colored car. The pass worked. There was just one car separating Dale Jarrett from victory—but that car belonged to Earnhardt, the Intimidator.

Through turn three, Jarrett urged his bright green machine to the inside of the Goodwrench Lumina. But Earnhardt fought back, crossing the line inches ahead of Jarrett as the white flag signaled the last lap of the race.

Jarrett was now getting worried. Jeff Gordon had chosen to draft up behind Earnhardt, and the two cars together threatened to blow by the 18 car. But then Geoffrey Bodine drafted up behind Jarrett, and coming off turn two, Dale Jarrett edged ahead of Dale Earnhardt. Jarrett maintained his perilous lead through turns three and four, and the cars thundered toward the checkered flag.

High above the track, in the CBS television booth, Daytona 500 broadcast anchor Ken Squier said to analyst Ned Jarrett, "Take your boy home, Ned."

And so, though his son could not hear his words, Ned Jarrett coached Dale into the record books.

"It's the Dale and Dale show as they come off of turn four. You know who I'm pulling for—it's Dale Jarrett," Ned admitted. "Bring her to the inside, Dale—don't let him get down there! He's going to make it! Dale Jarrett's going to win the Daytona 500!"

Among the first to congratulate Dale Jarrett as he coasted down pit road toward victory lane were the members of the Wood Brothers race team, a testament to Dale's popularity.

"From my perspective, this is the greatest victory a driver could have," Jarrett said as the implications of beating Dale Earnhardt for the huge win began to sink in. "I think Dale is the best driver to come into racing in a long, long time. He's done everything but win the Daytona 500. You almost have to feel sorry for him. So when you beat him, you know you have had your hands full."

Now a proven winner on the Winston Cup circuit, Jarrett and the Gibbs team began to place consistently in the top five. A season that boasted twelve such finishes to complement the Daytona win resulted in an improvement to fourth in the championship points.

Though the Interstate Batteries car returned to victory lane at Charlotte Motor Speedway in 1994, the overall performance of the team declined. By the end of 1994, the Gibbs operation was mired at sixteenth place in the points standings.

After weeks of trying to decide which way to go with his career, Dale Jarrett accepted an offer to drive for a rival Winston Cup Series team, one of the most respected operations in the NASCAR world: Robert Yates Racing.

Opposite: One of the greatest moments of any Winston Cup driver's career: standing in the victory lane of Daytona International Speedway as winner of the Daytona 500. This scene from 1993 was the first Daytona 500 victory for Jarrett, but it would by no means be his last...

CHAPTER FIVE

In 1994, Robert Yates' race team fielded the number 28 Ford Thunderbird, an imposing black Texaco-sponsored machine that had become one of the most respected—and feared—stock cars in the Winston Cup Series.

Yates' roots in the sport were deep. He had worked for the legendary Ford effort operated by Holman-Moody in the late 1960s, and then moved on to do engine work for Junior Johnson's team and drivers Bobby Allison and Cale Yarborough. In the fall of 1988, while working for Harry Ranier, Yates purchased the team from his boss. He was encouraged to do so by the team's driver, a young man from Alabama named Davey Allison.

Davey, the son of NASCAR legend Bobby Allison, had grown up playing with Dale Jarrett and the other children of NASCAR competitors. Seen as the next generation of his father's renowned "Alabama Gang," Davey made his mark in Winston Cup racing in a big way, winning twice in his rookie season against far more experienced veterans. His talent seemed limitless, and the partnership with Yates was a fruitful one.

Yates wasn't a man who was a team owner in name only; he had proven to be a mechanical genius, building his team's race powerplants with an innovative attention to detail. And teamed with young Davey, Robert Yates Racing had stormed into the ranks of the Winston Cup elite, capturing the 1992 Daytona 500 along the way and narrowly losing the championship to Alan Kulwicki.

Then tragedy struck. Davey Allison was killed in a helicopter accident in the summer of 1993. Though wounded emotionally, the Yates team rebounded with driver Ernie Irvan. He joined the team late in 1993, and his aggressive drives seemed to have the team poised for a Winston Cup championship in 1994. Irvan had already won three races that year when he suffered a

Pages 48-49: Dale Jarrett had substantial shoes to fill when he climbed behind the wheel of the number 28 Robert Yates Racing car. Yates drivers Davey Allison and Ernie Irvan had won many races and were fan favorites.

Left: The power of Robert Yates Racing's motors is legendary, and race fans expected to see sights like this, at Phoenix International Raceway in 1997, immediately after Dale Jarrett joined the Yates team.

Opposite: In reality, it was a struggle for Jarrett and the Yates team to find a winning combination in 1995. People began to question why Jarrett was having problems getting a proven winner into victory lane.

devastating crash in Michigan. Though Kenny Wallace substituted for the rest of the season, Yates needed a top driver for 1995 to fill in while Irvan recovered from near-fatal injuries. His choice was Dale Jarrett.

Having left the successful Joe Gibbs Racing operation, Jarrett was expected to be a smashing success in the black Yates Thunderbird. After all, he had the legendary power of the Robert Yates engines, the financial resources of a major sponsor, and a brilliant crew chief in Larry McReynolds, who had masterminded the on-track success achieved by Allison and Irvan.

It didn't work out the way anyone expected. Throughout 1995, the team found itself mired in mediocre performances. Instead of winning races, Jarrett struggled erratically to break into the top ten. Internal tensions boiled over into arguments among the team members. And to most observers, there was only one person who deserved the blame: Dale Jarrett. After all, weren't all the other team components exactly the same as in the glory days of Allison and Irvan?

At Charlotte Motor Speedway in May, Jarrett was forced to watch as another driver, Hut Stricklin, was put in the car during a practice session. Soon after, a heated meeting between Jarrett and the team brain trust was held. It could have resulted in Jarrett's resignation, but the driver refused to give up on the situation.

The meeting seemed to help clear the air. The team identified some subtle issues that had been affecting performance on the track, and the Thunderbird began to show flashes of running as it had in days of old. Finally, in July, at Pocono International Raceway in Pennsylvania, Dale Jarrett drove the Yates car to a win.

"Bad things were written, and my family heard people say really bad things—that basically Dale Jarrett couldn't drive a lick," Dale recalled of the days leading up to the win.

Most important, though, Yates' confidence in Jarrett had been reinforced. He was impressed by

Jarrett's determination to weather the difficult period and make the team a winner again. What no one knew was that Yates had been presented with an opportunity to turn his team into a two-car operation. Ernie Irvan would be returning to the 28 car,

Opposite: Robert Yates talks things over with his driver while a crew member at left analyzes spark plugs taken from Jarrett's car. "Reading" spark plugs can reveal how well a motor is running.

Below: Dale is actively involved in the setup of his stock cars, and his experience in the garage helps the Quality Care team prepare for every race.

Pages 54-55: The tight drafting of Daytona International Speedway finds Dale Jarrett in his number 88 car caught between Dave Marcis in front and Terry Labonte behind.

Above: The IROC series gives Dale Jarrett and other NASCAR stars the opportunity to test their skills against top drivers from other series, including motorsports legend Al Unser, Jr.

Opposite: Dale looks forward to a strong run at the historic Indianapolis Motor Speedway in 1996 after having won his second Daytona 500 earlier in the year.

but Yates knew just who he wanted behind the wheel the of the new number 88 in 1996: Dale Jarrett.

Sponsorship for the new team would come from Ford Motor Company through its Quality Care initiative, promoting customer satisfaction and owner loyalty. But even though the sponsorship dollars amounted to a significant figure, the fact that Yates was already fielding one successful team did not necessarily guarantee immediate success for the second team.

Adding to the uncertainty was the fact that Jarrett would be paired with Todd Parrott, who, after seventeen years as a Winston Cup crew member for various teams, would be making his debut as a crew chief. Todd's father, Buddy, was one of NASCAR's most respected crew chiefs. As the 1996

season dawned, Jarrett had to be hoping that Todd shared his father's renowned talents.

The team unloaded at Daytona and was fast right out of the truck. They were third fastest in qualifying for the Daytona 500, running a lap of 189.330 mph (304.6kph), just .036 mph (0.06kph) slower than Irvan in the other Yates car, and .180 mph (0.29kph) behind pole winner Dale Earnhardt.

Then, running in his first-ever appearance in the all-star Busch Clash race, Jarrett swept to victory, his Ford outpacing the Chevrolets of Sterling Marlin and Earnhardt.

But as Earnhardt could easily testify, winning the preliminaries leading up to the Daytona 500 was far from a guarantee of success in the big race. Yet as the laps wound down in the Daytona 500, the two drivers in the front of the pack created a sense of déjà vu—it was Dale and Dale, just as in 1993. And like that race three years earlier, Earnhardt was unable to propel himself past Dale Jarrett. With a new crew chief and a new team, Dale Jarrett had driven to his second Daytona 500 victory.

"It was a matter on the last lap of me getting a good run off of turn two," Jarrett explained after his big win. "I decided I was going to the middle of the racetrack, and that would give me room to maneuver to either side. I think he started high and then dove back low, but I was able to block both of those moves. The key was the Robert Yates engine that didn't allow him to get a run on me. I had enough horsepower to stay just ahead of him."

Jarrett knew that Todd Parrott had pulled off quite an achievement to get him to victory lane in their first Winston Cup showing.

"This was Todd's first race as a crew chief," Dale acknowledged, "and he did a fine job. This team was put together during the winter, so everybody deserves credit."

Much to the competition's dismay, the Daytona 500 was just the beginning of a strong season. Jarrett and company won NASCAR's longest race, the six-hundred-mile (965.4km) event at Charlotte Motor Speedway. That was followed by a win in Michigan, then a victory in the prestigious Brickyard 400 at Indianapolis Motor Speedway. Dale picked up a second win at Michigan, sweeping the track for the year. Though Terry Labonte won the Winston Cup championship, Jarrett's performance made it clear that NASCAR had a new superstar on the rise.

In 1997, having picked up the habit of sweeping both Winston Cup

races at a track, Jarrett won twice at Pocono International Raceway, Bristol Motor Speedway, Richmond International Raceway, and Charlotte Motor Speedway. Wins at South Carolina's Darlington Raceway, Atlanta Motor Speedway, and Phoenix International Raceway propelled Jarrett to the runner-up position in the championship race, falling just fourteen points shy of Jeff Gordon's total.

In 1998, Jarrett's Robert Yates Racing team swept Alabama's Talladega Superspeedway and won again at Darlington and Delaware's Dover Downs International Speedway. At the end of the season, Jarrett had once again fallen just short in the championship battle, finishing third.

Racing in the 1998 Brickyard 400, the Quality Care Ford had obviously been the class of the field. Jarrett could drive the car wherever he needed to, and it quickly became apparent that the 88 car was destined for victory lane—until a miscalculation on fuel mileage led to the Ford running out of gas at a crucial stage in the race.

The incident at Indianapolis resulted in victory being snatched from Dale Jarrett. It was the kind of mistake that could derail a run at the Winston Cup Series championship. If the Quality Care team was ever to see its driver crowned NASCAR's champion, mistakes like the one that had cost them the Brickyard 400 had to be eliminated.

Left: Two Dales–Jarrett (left) and Earnhardt–share a lighthearted moment in the Winston Cup garage area...

Opposite: ...Behind the wheel, though, it's all business. Jarrett focuses on the job at hand in 1997.

CHAPTER SIX

As the Winston Cup Series arrived under the Florida skies for the events leading up to the season-opening 1999 Daytona 500, Dale Jarrett had made a convincing argument for his status as championship contender. The problem was that every year there are always numerous contenders, but just one champion. Though the Quality Care Ford team was a smoothly functioning race operation, and always a threat to win any Winston Cup event, if they wanted to beat Jeff Gordon and the other teams striving for the top, they would have to find a way to improve a tiny bit more.

One thing was clear in the results of the Bud Shootout all-star race one week before the Daytona 500: all of the Winston Cup cars had a shot at winning NASCAR's biggest race. The twenty-five-lap shootout for the fastest qualifiers of the 1998 season featured a top-five finishing order of Ford, Chevrolet, Pontiac, Chevrolet, and Ford. But whereas Mark Martin had used his drafting skills to nudge his Ford Taurus across the finish line just ahead of Ken Schrader to win the event, Dale Jarrett had placed eighth in the fifteen-car field and had never really been in contention to win.

Then again, most race teams that qualify to compete in the Bud Shootout generally have separate cars for the "dash for cash," wisely choosing not to risk their Daytona 500 cars in the shootout's brief, heated competition.

The fact that Jarrett had the eighteenth fastest speed in the first round of Daytona 500 qualifying the day before the Bud Shootout wasn't necessarily a cause for alarm, either. Most race teams seek

Pages 60-61: A crew member fastens the protective window net as Dale Jarrett prepares to enter into competition.

Left: Crew chief Todd Parrott, clutching his ever-present notes, assesses the situation with his driver.

Opposite: Each track of the Winston Cup Series presents a challenge to be overcome, from the high banks of Daytona to the sweeping flat turns seen here at the new Homestead-Miami Speedway.

only a decent run since the actual 500 starting order is determined in the 125-mile (201.1km) qualifying races held three days before the big race. And in those qualifying races, many drivers run conservative races as well. After all, what would be the point of wrecking your Daytona 500 car with an over-aggressive run trying to qualify?

But if anyone expected Jarrett to run a conservative 125-mile (201.1km) race, his expectations were turned around by the sight of the blue Ford running at the front of the pack as the laps wound down. Though Dale Earnhardt streaked across the finish line first—winning his tenth straight 125-mile (201.1km) Daytona 500 qualifying race—the Fords of Jeremy Mayfield and Dale Jarrett were breathing down the Intimidator's back. The margin of victory was just .251 second.

Dale Jarrett, Todd Parrott, and the entire Quality Care team seemed to be in great shape for the Daytona 500. Dale's Taurus was running well through the tricky air currents of 200-mph (321.8kph) drafting, proving that his car could go to the front and, more important, stay there.

And then came Kenny Irwin.

It was more than halfway through the Daytona 500, and Jarrett had been running well. But three-wide competition is always a treacherous proposition at Daytona, and that was just the position Jarrett found himself in as a pack of cars thundered down the long backstretch of Daytona International Speedway. Joining Jarrett in the chancy side-by-side dance were longtime veteran Bill Elliott and newcomer Irwin, Jarrett's teammate in the Robert Yates stable.

Above: Ned Jarrett gives his son a hug after a convincing win by the Yates team in the 1999 Brickyard 400 at Indianapolis Motor Speedway.

Opposite: Many observers wondered if Dale Jarrett's 1999 level of performance would carry over into 2000. They got their answer when the team roared to a win in the first race of the season—the 2000 Daytona 500.

Irwin had seemed to be a great choice to join the Yates team in 1998 when Ernie Irvan parted ways with the number 28 car operation. But Irwin's rookie season had been considered by many a disaster, and there had even been some dissention among the crew about Irwin's performances and lifestyle away from the track. Irwin was determined to make a strong showing in the Daytona 500.

As the cars neared turn three, Irwin's black Taurus seemed to slightly nudge Jarrett's Ford. At 200 mph (321.8kph), a nudge is all it takes to cause a crash.

"He was three-wide in the center going down the back straightaway," Irwin later said of Jarrett. "I don't know if we actually touched or if the air just got off his spoiler and he spun. I have no idea, but I feel very, very bad about it, if it was my fault."

Pages 66-67: *One advantage Dale Jarrett had throughout the 1999 season was the pit work of his team. Their athletic performances frequently insured that Jarrett's car was serviced and back on the track ahead of the competition.*

Above: *Todd Parrott searches for a way to squeeze out more speed as Dale Jarrett takes a brief break. The hours of fine-tuning leading up to a race are crucial if a team wants a chance at victory.*

Opposite: *When the checkered flag waves and your car is out front, it's time to momentarily forget the hard work and savor the win. Jarrett's team went to victory lane four times in 1999.*

Regardless of fault, the consequences of the resulting melee were clear. Dale Jarrett's car went airborne during the ensuing chaos, sliding up off the track apron and into the path of the pack that was racing just behind. When the smoke cleared, twelve top contenders had been involved. Mercifully, Jarrett's Ford had landed on all four tires. The dejected driver took off his helmet and walked away from his battered car. Kenny Irwin went on to finish third.

Finishing the Daytona 500 in thirty-seventh place is not what the 88 team had in mind. If they were to compete for the championship, they had to overcome the disastrous start. But every team suffers bad luck at some point in the season, and they were willing to accept the fact that their bad luck had come early in the year. Now, as the Winston Cup Series moved on and the season began to settle in, it was time to make some good luck.

At North Carolina Speedway, Mark Martin powered to victory in the second points race of the season, with more than a full second separating him from runner-up Dale Jarrett. But to the 88 team, that second-place finish must have seemed almost as good as a win after the Daytona disaster.

Next, for just the second time, the Winston Cup Series raced at Las Vegas Motor Speedway. Most teams rely on volumes of notes collected from years of running at tracks on the NASCAR circuit, but at a newer speedway it can be hit or miss. The 88 team didn't miss entirely, but finishing eleventh was far from perfection.

"There never was a situation where we thought we got the car right," Jarrett admitted.

Back at the familiar environs of Atlanta Motor Speedway, trouble was still rearing its head. Pit crew miscues were complicated by a faulty jack. Jarrett himself was penalized fifteen seconds for running too fast on pit road. Nobody was happy with how the Yates engine was running. And still, the team came home with a top-five.

"We worked on it and got it better," Jarrett noted, "but fifth place is pretty good considering everything that we went through."

The race team knew that the ability to make the most of a poor-handling race car while overcoming adversity during pit stops was essential to a championship run. Things were coming together for the 88 team.

Though Jarrett had won the spring race at South Carolina's historic Darlington Raceway in both 1997 and 1998, his quest for a third straight win in the event fell short by three positions. Still, it was a good run on a strange day that saw Jeff Burton win the race when rain stopped the event— just after Burton crashed. Had the rain not come at that exact moment, Burton surely would have had to pit for repairs. With the racing gods on Burton's side that day, Jarrett had to settle for his fourth-place finish. He headed for Texas sixth in the points standings.

It seemed that Jarrett might be destined for his elusive first win of the season at Texas Motor Speedway, but "Texas Terry" Labonte had other ideas for the outcome of the race at his home-state track.

With the race nearing its conclusion, Dale Jarrett had placed his Taurus at the front of the field. But Labonte was charging. He closed on the back bumper of Jarrett, and Dale desperately tried to keep the Hendrick Motorsports Monte Carlo behind him. But Jarrett got hung up trying to pass a lapped car. He was forced to crack the throttle, and it was all Labonte needed to get by with just twelve laps remaining. Jarrett never could catch Terry again.

"Terry just got up high and got a run on the outside," Jarrett commented, "and there was nothing I could do." Dale's high finishing position in Texas, though, elevated the Yates team to third in the points.

It was on to Tennessee's Bristol Motor Speedway for the 88 team, still chasing their first

Opposite: The focus of a champion: intensity and dedication are the hallmarks of a successful run at the Winston Cup championship.

Above: The Robert Yates Racing team rolls the number 88 Ford Taurus to the grid for qualifying at the 1999 Michigan 400.

win of the season. At Bristol, a high-banked, high-speed half-mile (0.8km) track, just finishing the race is often considered something of a victory. When accidents happen on the narrow track, drivers have little room for evasive maneuvers. But Jarrett drove a smart race to come home in third.

"It was a good day for us," Jarrett allowed. "We had to adjust on the car a lot, and finally got it to where it was pretty good, especially on long runs. To get a top-five here is pretty good. We gained some points, that's the main thing." Indeed they did, climbing into second in the standings and

closing to within fifty-two points of leader Jeff Burton.

The short-track portion of the season continued at Virginia's Martinsville Speedway. Jarrett had a poor qualifying effort and started deep in the field. His Taurus was not the most competitive of cars when the race began, but Todd Parrott and the crew worked hard to fine-tune the stock car all day. When the checkered flag fell, Jarrett had clawed his way to eighth place. Under the circumstances, a top-ten was something to be happy about.

Now the Winston Cup stars journeyed from the short half-mile (0.8km) of Martinsville to NASCAR's largest track, Alabama's imposing 2.66-mile (4.3km) Talladega Superspeedway.

Most drivers will admit that Dale Earnhardt is a master at Talladega, but the other Dale isn't too bad either, having won the last time the series had competed in Alabama. This time, though, the Intimidator reigned supreme. Right behind him, Dale Jarrett did all he could to catch Earnhardt. But Mark Martin wasn't able to get close enough to Jarrett to give the 88 car the aerodynamic push it needed to catch the black Goodwrench Chevrolet. Jarrett had come in second again.

At California Speedway, it was up to the crew to salvage the day after Jarrett's Taurus sustained damage when a tire failed.

"You just have to keep battling," Jarrett said, and that's what the team did to claim fifth place, hanging on to second in the points.

The consistency the team had shown put them on the right track to contend for the championship. But drivers want to win, not just run consistently. Despite multiple top-fives, the season was four months old and Dale had yet to visit victory lane. That all changed at Richmond International Raceway in Virginia.

While others pushed their car setups to the limit, Todd Parrott devised a careful setup that did the trick on the D-shaped racetrack.

"We were just taking our time and making small adjustments," a happy Jarrett said after the win. "We made a small adjustment at the end, and the car was the best it had been all night. That's what makes Todd Parrott so good."

When a driver is happy with his car, he knows he can win; Jarrett was very happy with this car.

Right: A successful pit stop is an intricate ballet of tire mounting and refueling—performed in less than sixteen seconds.

"Todd just made the right call at the end. The last set of tries really made the car hook up off the corner," Jarrett enthused. "On that last run I could have driven anywhere. If I had had to make another pit stop, I couldn't have told him how to make it any better." And with the win, Jarrett and company moved into the lead in the points for the first time.

Dale fell from the Winston all-star race at Lowe's Motor Speedway (formerly Charlotte Motor Speedway) in North Carolina after tangling with Bobby Hamilton, but the short race doesn't count in the points. The six-hundred-mile (965.4km) race at the same track a week later definitely does. Jarrett hung on for fifth place in NASCAR's longest race, but a cause for concern was the winner of the event, Jeff Burton.

Burton and Jarrett had battled for the points lead all season, and Burton's win pulled him to within a handful of points of Jarrett. Dale may have been glad the next stop on the schedule was Dover, a race that he had won in 1998.

Jarrett finished in fifth place yet again at Dover, and the best Burton could manage was eighth. The points gap began to widen.

Below: Dale Jarrett rolls along in the outside line as he prepares to start the 1999 Brickyard 400. At the end of the day, he had won his second race at the famous Indianapolis Motor Speedway.

To drive home the point, Dale dominated at Michigan, winning for the second time as the halfway point of the season neared.

"My car was incredible," Jarrett said. "That's the only way I know to describe it. It was the best race car I've ever been in."

So dominant was the 88 car that the fans weren't the only ones bored with watching Jarrett thrash the field.

"It was a pretty boring day," runner-up Jeff Gordon admitted. "I couldn't even see him. I saw him when he was just letting off there at the end to make it look good, but he was untouchable."

Jeff Burton finished in third and shared Gordon's frustration at Jarrett's power.

"I got excited one time, because I could see him," Burton noted. "When I came off two, he was going off into four, and I told them, 'Yeah, I can see him!'"

Burton also saw his point deficit increase despite a strong run.

Jeff Burton fell further behind when he crashed at Pocono International Raceway, while Jarrett maintained his steady pace of top-ten finishes, taking third place at the Pennsylvania track. The winner of the race, Bobby Labonte, passed Burton in the points. But Dale still had the lead, just the way he liked it—and there were no plans to start racing conservatively.

"If we start getting conservative or something, who knows what could happen," Dale said at Pocono. "We're just racing to win."

Jarrett credited his pit crew for his next top-ten finish, a sixth-place run in California at the road course at Sears Point Raceway. And so the Winston Cup season moved into its second half, with a return to Daytona International Speedway.

The traditional four-hundred-mile (643.6km) summer race is now run under the lights, but the cooler evening temperatures do little to chill the action on the superspeedway. More so than at Talladega, Daytona demands a car that will handle well. On July 3, Dale Jarrett had just that kind of car.

As the race unfolded, getting the car to react properly to the tires became critical. Todd Parrott adjusted the tire pressures, which can change how a car reacts in competition. His experience led to his making the right call, one that led to victory at Daytona, but not before Jarrett faced his old superspeedway nemesis.

On the final pit stop, Jarrett took on gas only, getting out of the pits ahead of Rusty Wallace, who led the most laps in the event. But Dale Earnhardt took on fuel and two fresh tires, and he began carving his way toward Jarrett. As the Intimidator moved forward, other competitors drafted with him.

"Earnhardt seems to get more help," Jarrett said, "because guys know he's going to the front, so they want to latch onto him to improve their position. It's not that people want to help him win, they want to help themselves improve their positions, so he gets a lot of help in that way. When I saw that start happening, I knew he was going to be a factor."

He was a factor, but he simply ran out of time before he could catch Jarrett. With four laps to go,

the caution flag waved. Jarrett would win the race—if he had enough fuel. Cruising around the superspeedway at reduced speed, Earnhardt crowded Jarrett, making it clear that if Jarrett's car faltered he'd be more than happy to accept the win. He never got the chance. Dale Jarrett had won for the third time, adding to his points cushion.

"We've got a lot of confidence right now," Jarrett said. "As far as getting conservative, I don't think that's going to happen. We want to get as big a lead as we can and enjoy it. Hopefully, the end of the season will get here soon."

Dale's quest for the championship had taken him to the top of the points chase, but at New Hampshire International Speedway in Loudon, a run-in was in store with the reigning Winston Cup champion.

Rookie Tony Stewart had garnered the most attention on a sunny day, seemingly on his way to his first win after a sensational performance in his Joe Gibbs Pontiac. But Stewart ran out of fuel with just two laps remaining. The lead was inherited by Jeff Burton, but a scramble was about to ensue among Kenny Wallace, Jeff Gordon, and Jarrett.

As Jarrett attempted to get by Wallace, contact was initiated by Gordon, who had closed on the Quality Care Taurus. The result was that Jarrett got out of shape, and Gordon shot by the 88 car in his rainbow Monte Carlo. Burton went on to win for the third straight time at the Northern track, followed by Wallace, Gordon, and Jarrett. Immediately after the race, Dale and Jeff had a heated exchange of words.

"It was just a little bit of rubbing out there," Jarrett later diplomatically insisted. "We'll see each other again. We've got a lot of racing to do, but we had a good day. That's what we needed to do, have a good finish."

But when pressed on his incident with Gordon, Jarrett issued an ominous declaration: "If he'd hit me once, that's one thing. But he hit me three times. If he wants to make it a war, we can do that."

"I got into the back of him going into three on the last lap," Gordon countered. "He didn't like the way I made the pass, but I didn't like the way he ran me down low, either. I got up underneath him on that last lap, and he ran me all the way down into the apron. When we got to three, there wasn't enough room. I got into the back of him and made the pass. If he wouldn't have blocked me, I wouldn't have touched him, but once he blocked me all the way down low, I figured that was fair game."

If Jarrett's temper was up in the wake of his battle with Gordon, so was his points lead. Another top-five found him more than two hundred points ahead of Mark Martin, Jeff Burton, and Bobby Labonte.

Labonte knew he had to make a charge through the points soon if he had a chance at catching Jarrett, and he put his plan in action by winning in dominating form at the Winston Cup Series' return

Opposite: A perfect pit stop means nothing if the driver can't get the car back onto the track. Here Dale Jarrett narrowly avoids contact with Mark Martin.

to Pocono. The problem was that his gain was incremental: Dale Jarrett finished just behind Labonte's green Pontiac in second place.

And so it was off to Indiana to race at historic Indianapolis Motor Speedway. Dale Jarrett was champion in the Brickyard 400 in 1996, and a repeat performance in 1999 could have a demoralizing effect on his fellow competitors. If he could win at the huge, flat track and add to his already considerable points margin, a championship for the 88 car would seem ever more likely.

Dale Jarrett won, and did it in resounding fashion. Not only did he power to a margin of victory of more than three seconds after restarting the race with just thirteen laps remaining, he also set a new record for most laps led in the Brickyard 400 by keeping his blue Taurus out front for 116 circuits.

"The hardest part when you have a lead like I had is to stay consistent," Jarrett noted. "Obviously, you don't want to make a mistake and it's easy to

get out there and maybe get a little complacent. But Todd is good at giving me times and letting me know. Of course, for the majority of the race I had someone pretty close behind me, so I could kind of gauge off that, to determine if they were catching me in a corner.

"There's no chance of losing concentration. You don't do that because to get around this place you really have to perform well in each corner and I think that challenge keeps you on your toes."

Of course, Dale gave credit to the exceptional stock car that he drove to victory: "This is the same car we used last year. It's an incredible car. You saw it, you know it."

Below: An Indianapolis Motor Speedway tradition is observed here as the Quality Care crew gives thanks to the track that gave them a victory in the 1999 Brickyard 400.

Opposite: Winning a Winston Cup championship demands a season-long effort and total dedication week in and week out, a lesson Dale Jarrett learned early on in his NASCAR career.

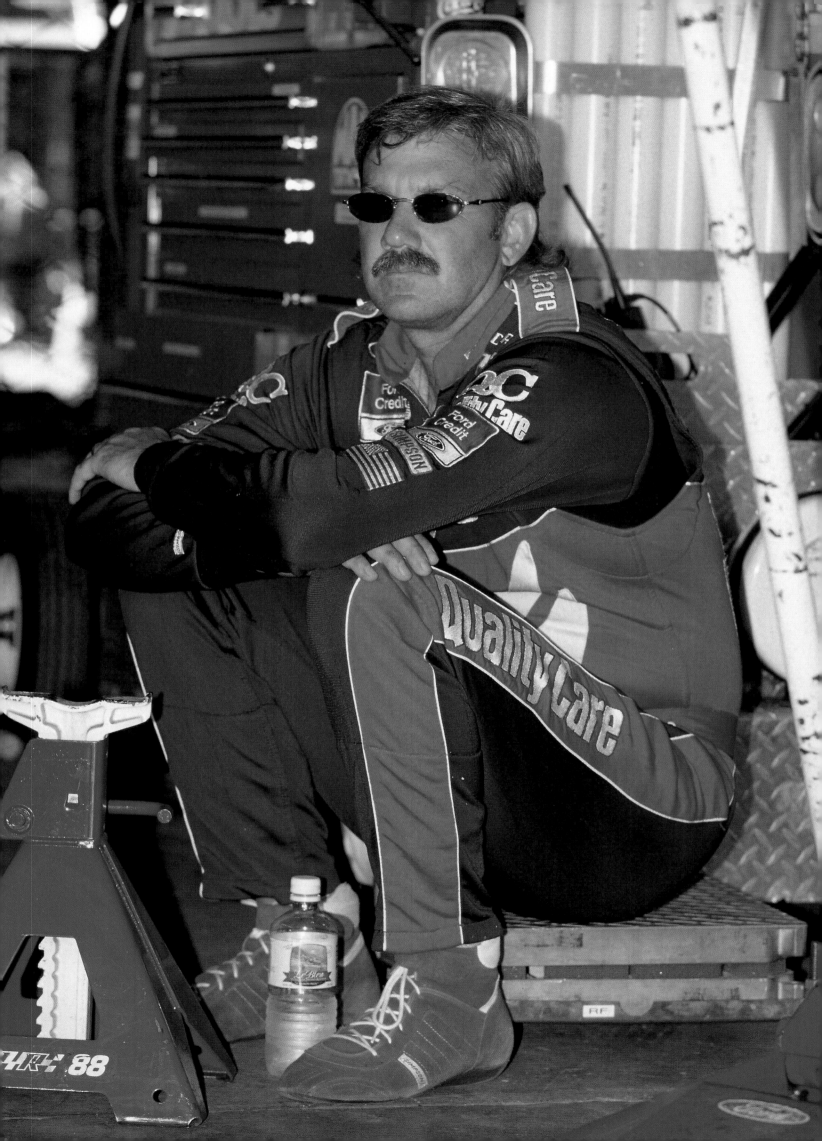

With a points margin approaching three hundred, Dale Jarrett, Todd Parrott, and the Quality Care team were looking like Winston Cup champs. And the strong runs kept on coming: fourth at Watkins Glen International in New York and Michigan International Speedway. But the Jarrett Express derailed at Tennessee's Bristol Motor Speedway, when Dale crashed and headed home credited with thirty-eighth place. The next week a poorly timed pit stop hurt when rain ended the race early at Darlington Raceway in South Carolina. Gambling that the race would be restarted, Dale took on four tires and returned to the track in sixteenth, the finishing position he was credited with when NASCAR called the event.

Mark Martin began to entertain thoughts of catching Jarrett. After all, he made up almost 150 points of Jarrett's three-hundred-point lead and had accomplished it in just two races. But the experienced Yates crew kept their cool and helped Dale back to the top with a third-place finish at Richmond International Raceway. Jarrett stumbled again at the return to New Hampshire, finishing eighteenth, but Martin couldn't capitalize; he finished just one position in front of Dale.

Martin won at Dover Downs International Speedway, by more than a full second over Tony Stewart, but it did little good—Jarrett came in third. Tenth place at Virginia's Martinsville Speedway added to Jarrett's lead when Martin's best was sixteenth. Bobby Labonte took advantage of Martin's problems to move into second in points. Labonte was runner-up and Martin was sixth at North Carolina's Lowe's Motor Speedway, but Jarrett shadowed both in seventh and left the Charlotte-area speedway with a commanding 222-point lead. It began to look as though Labonte and Martin would just be fighting it out for second.

That impression was reinforced when Jarrett streaked across the finish line just behind winner Dale Earnhardt at Alabama's Talladega Superspeedway. With just four races left in the season, Jarrett's lead was a comfortable 246 points. Fourth place at North Carolina Speedway brought the title closer.

"We're getting a lot closer now," Jarrett cautiously allowed. "As we knock these races off and don't lose any points or gain a few, it's looking a lot more promising. This team has worked awful hard to get to this point and we're excited about the prospect for these next three. It's a lot more exciting time for us. These guys, I hope, are enjoying it."

The entire team enjoyed a sixth-place at Phoenix International Raceway, leaving Jarrett in the enviable position of simply

needing to finish eighth or better at Florida's Homestead-Miami Speedway.

Dale had a so-so qualifying run at the track. It was the NASCAR Winston Cup Series' first visit to the flat 1.5-mile (2.4km) speedway, and like all the teams, the Robert Yates Racing 88 car team had to analyze how their car needed to be set up for the race to come. When the race started, Jarrett was still uncertain how he would fare.

"We really didn't know what was going to happen as the race went on with our car," Jarrett said. "I think that caused a little bit more excitement for us with the unknown. We started out, the car was a little bit loose, so we just kind of made our way around for that first set of tires and made some adjustments and got the car a little better."

A little better?

"We just had to stay out of trouble," Dale admitted. "We had a definite top-five car and that's what we had to do."

When the race ended three hours after the green flag waved, Dale Jarrett had driven a smart and careful race. He finished in fifth place.

Dale Jarrett was the 1999 NASCAR Winston Cup Series champion.

CHAPTER SEVEN

From the top of his blue Ford Taurus, Dale Jarrett surveyed the scene before him at Homestead-Miami Speedway, a broad smile on his face. At last, the years of effort had paid off. No longer just another championship contender, Jarrett was NASCAR's newest champion.

Though he could have quite happily stayed atop his automotive perch for much longer, Jarrett was eventually coaxed down to comment on his momentous achievement.

"Coming out and winning one race is nothing like what you have to do for an entire season, especially with the competition this day and time," the jubilant Jarrett said. "I think you have to realize that it takes time for us to learn, for us to work together, to get all the people in the right places and that's what this is about in our fourth year."

As race fans might have expected, even in his time of celebration Jarrett—as only the second son to join his father as a NASCAR champion—paid sincere tribute to the drivers who preceded him in the Robert Yates organization, recognizing the importance of roots in his sport.

"We want to look back and thank two guys that helped bring this organization to where it is, Davey Allison for getting all this started and then Ernie Irvan for his contribution in making this a winning operation," Dale stated. "Without their talents and their support, we'd have never gotten this far and we just want to make sure those guys are remembered for being a part of this."

Jarrett was quick to elaborate on the crucial foundation that Allison had helped to build when he convinced Robert Yates to take the plunge as a Winston Cup owner.

"He's the one who sat with Robert and started this whole thing," Dale acknowledged. "The success they had, the organization that they built from the very beginning. None of this would have ever happened if it wasn't for Davey and it's unfortunate that he was taken, not only from our sport, but from a lot of people's lives because of the person that he was. There's no doubt in my mind that he's had a huge hand in this, along with Ernie and what he was able to do and accomplish and keep things going at Robert Yates Racing. Davey Allison was a very special person and we know that's someone we've had on our side this whole time."

Though Dale Jarrett honorably chose to remember the past at this most special of times, there was still an immediate future to be dealt with: the final race of 1999, at Atlanta Motor Speedway. After the celebrating, and with the pressure of hoarding points removed, the 88 team was relaxed and ready to race.

After starting from the tenth position, Dale Jarrett motored toward the front of the pack, and as he had done for most of the 1999 season, he placed himself firmly in contention by running in the top five the majority of the afternoon, and leading twice in the race's late stages. When the check-

Pages 82-83: Throughout the days leading up to the 2000 Daytona 500, the Quality Care team functioned with the confidence of champions.

Opposite: Replacing Kenny Irwin as the driver of the second Robert Yates entry for 2000 was Ricky Rudd, seen here talking with his new teammate Dale Jarrett at Daytona.

ered flag waved, Jarrett was in second place. "He drove his heart out and he didn't have to do that," crew chief Todd Parrott said in admiration of Jarrett's run. "He had no reason to do it. We had the championship locked up, but if he couldn't win the race, he wanted to finish second, because that's the way he's been all year long."

The race was won by Bobby Labonte in the Joe Gibbs Racing Pontiac. Labonte was strong all year, building on his experience of seasons past and winding up second in the championship points. Will Bobby Labonte be the biggest threat to wrestle away the championship from Dale Jarrett in 2000?

That was a question sure to be argued by race fans across the country in the cold winter months leading up to the Daytona 500 in February. But while the fans were looking forward to the return of the cars to Daytona's high banks, Dale Jarrett left Atlanta Motor Speedway looking forward to a trip to New York City for the Winston Cup awards banquet.

Days of activities led up to the banquet itself, held on December 3, 1999. The gathering—in recent years broadcast live on the ESPN cable sports network—gives everyone a chance to speak about how important the Winston Cup championship is, including Dale's wife, Kelley.

"As the wife of a NASCAR Winston Cup competitor, people often tell me they can't imagine how we wives handle the hectic schedules on the cir-

Opposite: Dale Jarrett fended off all competition at Daytona, qualifying on the pole and winning the Daytona 500. It was a week of domination by the Robert Yates Racing team.

cuit," Kelley said. "I tell them our lives are no more challenging than theirs, that we're probably on autopilot from October on, but it is a different kind of challenge. And with the tremendous increasing popularity our sport has received in the last five to ten years, it has brought more demands on everyone involved."

She then alluded to her sons and daughters.

"These drivers, car owners, crew chiefs, engine builders, and I do mean stellar crewmen, are heroes to all their fans, as well they should be. But first and foremost they're heroes to the little Zacharys, Natalees, Karsyns, and the big Jasons of this world."

When Dale took his turn at the podium, with his parents in the audience, he also mentioned the importance of family.

"Family is extremely important to me, and I am honored and fortunate to say that mine is a true champion," Jarrett said. "They have supported me through the best and worst of times. Mom and Dad, thanks for your many years of guidance and support. Your willingness to help others and the examples you set for us being leaders are what made me, my entire family very proud."

Despite the distractions that come with being a top NASCAR star, Jarrett kept his focus on what was truly important.

"I would have to say that 1999 has been an incredible year in my life for many reasons," Jarrett stated. "And here are just a few of them: I was able to attend a Dallas Mavericks basketball game earlier this year and receive a team jersey. I was able to throw out the first pitch at Tigers Stadium in Detroit. Meeting Tour de France winner Lance

Armstrong, who is a true inspiration to everyone. Playing golf with a true legend, Arnold Palmer. And, oh yes, winning my second Brickyard 400, but most of all, winning this NASCAR Winston Cup championship."

Todd Parrott took the stage, giving a peek into the unique communication between driver and crew chief that must be part of a team foundation if championship dreams are to ever become a reality.

"Dale and I usually finish each other's sentences," Parrott noted. "And I bet that's scary to some of you. But that's a big part of how we got up here tonight. Dale never fails to give me credit for our accomplishments. And let me tell you, Dale Jarrett is a true champion in every sense of the word."

But Dale wanted to stress to the whole sports world the importance of his crew. Addressing his crew members, Jarrett made his point clear: "You are all very special, and now the world knows what I have known for five years, that everyone at Robert Yates Racing is a champion."

While Dale Jarrett would probably be the first to insist that the pride and prestige of a championship season is reward enough, it's worth noting that Dale had nearly $3.5 million in race winnings, plus almost another $3 million in awards money. His total jackpot for the 1999 season was an astounding $6,649,956. Not too bad for someone whose first racing paycheck was $35 for a ninth-place finish in 1977.

In the weeks after the banquet, as the 2000 season approached, Jarrett had time to reflect on some of the changes brought on by the championship.

"Even going to the dry cleaners, you have to sign stuff now," Jarrett said. "You can't just pick up your clothes; you've got to autograph this before you can get your clothes.

"One of the coolest things to me is going to happen here in a couple of weeks. I'm going to get to go to Augusta and play. I'm sure good weather is getting ready to end. It might be 20 degrees, but I told them as long as the golf course was open, I was going. Just good opportunities. I've actually had two or three opportunities to go play, so I'm going to take each and every one of them if I can."

But while the recreational opportunities presented by being a NASCAR Winston Cup champion are appealing, there is no stopping the clock. While Jarrett thought of golf in January, he worried about the Daytona 500 and a new season in which he would be the defending champion.

"I guess, right now if I had to look at everything, I'd say we are once again a little bit behind," Jarrett admitted. "I think Todd would agree with me in saying that we don't have a lot of cars built right now, we have our two cars for Daytona that are in pretty good shape. We go there this coming Thursday and Friday to test. The test that we had at Talladega, we did with one car and it went pretty well. It's still hard to judge when you just have the Fords there. We have to see what the GM cars will do at the first of the week and that will give us a better idea, but I think we have a good car.

"The changes that were made for the 2000 Taurus seem like they're going to be pretty good for us on the racetrack, but again, a lot of it is because of wind tunnel numbers that we've seen that gives us a little bit of optimism there," Jarrett continued in his customary fashion.

"Again, we are behind in building cars, with having 10 straight weeks to start the season out, or 10 straight races there, it makes it a little more difficult.

"In trying to win the championship last year, we stayed totally focused on that and we didn't get started on 2000. Of course, we didn't have the pieces and the templates to get started either, so we may not be any further behind than a lot of others. But, you'd have to say that with Chevrolet having their car there for a while that they could work on; and, of course, Pontiac doesn't have something new, so they have to be looking pretty good and pretty excited to know that everybody else is kind of struggling around." Cautious and even-handed as ever, Jarrett was being realistic.

Still, Jarrett was confident that the necessary work would be done, and that his crew had deserved some time off after the championship charge: "I think we'll be in good shape once we get started and it takes a little bit of overtime. We tried to give our guys time to enjoy the championship, not only in New York, but a little bit of time to enjoy it with their families around Christmas. Then, whenever they come back, you realize that by taking that time off, you've created a lot of work in a short period of time. So, that's kind of what's going on now."

Although winning the championship was a goal realized, Jarrett knows that he is now the target

Below: Dale Jarrett crosses the start/finish line to win the first Daytona 500 of the twenty-first century, in the process passing a fleet of rescue vehicles (on the scene to deal with a late-race crash) and adding an exclamation mark to the previous season's championship run.

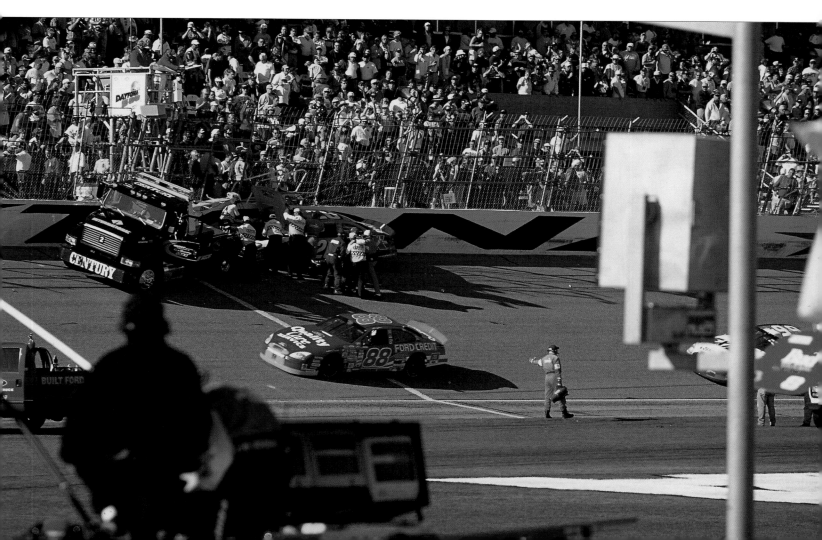

that everyone will be aiming for. The impression that a champion enters a season with a big advantage is not necessarily accurate—in fact, it could be the opposite.

"I don't know that there's really an advantage, because all of that's out the window now and this is a totally new season and everybody is at the same place right now," Jarrett noted. "Nobody has any points and everybody believes they can win races and win the championship. But, I think what it does is it gives us a confidence level certainly that helps us and puts us a little ahead of others that

Above: The demands on the time of the Winston Cup champion are myriad. Here Dale Jarrett has a rare moment of solitude at Las Vegas Motor Speedway in March 2000.

haven't won it and maybe others that haven't won it recently. So, you have that.

"The knowledge of what it takes to win a championship, to understand the things that you have to do, the pressures you have to go through and handling that; yeah, that's definitely an advantage, because there's a lot more involved there than what I ever anticipated. I think that's what gave me a greater appreciation again for Dale Earnhardt and Richard Petty and Jeff Gordon in winning multiple championships and what they were able to accomplish there. There are some advantages to being the champion and going through all of that, but as far as preparation-wise or race team–wise, I don't know that it gives you any there, or even on track."

Late in the 1999 season, defending Winston Cup champion Jeff Gordon lost not only his brilliant crew chief, Ray Evernham, who left to build Chrysler's new Winston Cup program, but also most of his race-day pit crew when they elected to leave Hendrick Motorsports as a group. Jarrett knows that keeping his crew happy is crucial to keeping a championship-caliber team on track.

"I certainly think winning races and championships helps somewhat, but, obviously, that's not the total key because it doesn't always ensure that you'll keep them together," Jarrett said. "But, we've tried to make sure that our employees at Robert Yates Racing are people that are happy and enjoy their jobs. We give them a good place to work; their bonuses are good; as we do well, they do well also. And I think that we all realize that that's what keeps people around. We try to make sure that we're very competitive price-wise for their salaries, but again, I think that giving them opportunities to work and be specialized in their field is something that they may not get at other places… they might just be kind of in a group, and we've tried to make it pretty specialized for them in their jobs and what they do and make more time for them with their

families to enjoy the monies that they make. We've tried to set each one of them and ask them if there's something about the place that they would change or in their working conditions that they would change, so we've taken a lot of extra time.

"Robert and Todd have spent a lot of time at that, I've spent as much time as I could with them, just making sure that the guys are happy and that they want to continue to work hard for us. There are no guarantees; you can't keep everybody. If we can keep the key people, we're going to be able to bring in others."

Like Dale Jarrett, many of today's established Winston Cup stars struggled in uncompetitive cars while they did everything they could to put down roots in NASCAR's elite stock car racing series. But when Jeff Gordon broke into the Winston Cup Series in 1992 and 1993 at the wheel of a Hendrick Motorsports Lumina, with the best equipment and a major sponsorship backing him, the idea of a rookie winning Winston Cup races wasn't so far-fetched. When rookie Tony Stewart won three races in 1999, a convincing argument was made for the attainability of instant success. Dale Jarrett knows that the competition will now be more fierce than ever with new drivers like Dale Earnhardt Jr. and Matt Kenseth wheeling Winston Cup stock cars.

"These young guys and the opportunities they have and the impact they're going to have on our sport, they all have a lot of talent and I think each one of them will find days that they're going to have opportunities to win races," Jarrett speculated. "I think certainly with Dale's experience and Matt's experience winning races in the Busch Series that you have to look at those guys and that they have really good opportunities. They have good cars and they have a lot of talent.... Five hundred miles is a long time to put everything together. Race tracks change, the cars change, and that's something they'll have to work and learn to deal with, but I think this is probably the best rookie class that we've ever seen come into Winston Cup."

When the season finally got underway, that rookie class could have learned almost everything they needed to know by watching Dale Jarrett's performance at the 2000 Daytona 500. Dale swept the pole position in the qualifying races, won a qualifying race for the all-star Bud Shootout, won the shootout itself, and then won his third Daytona 500. Sharing in the glory was Todd Parrott and the entire Robert Yates Racing crew, who heroically repaired serious damage to the 88 car that was sustained during the final practice session just hours before the Daytona 500. Simply put, Jarrett and his team absolutely dominated Daytona Speedweeks.

No matter how strong the competition is in 2000, though, Dale Jarrett is now focused on winning a second championship, as father Ned Jarrett did more than thirty years ago. Though he'd like to match that feat, the motivation for running hard to the title again comes not from familial competition, but from the burning desire to succeed in racing—a desire that has characterized Dale Jarrett's career.

"I don't want to stay in another room besides the one I did in the Waldorf. That's enough for me. I think it's just that success breeds success," Dale Jarrett explained. "You win this and that's what you want to do again. You've almost come to the

Above: Sometimes a picture is worth a thousand words, and sometimes a simple gesture can say it all: Dale Jarrett was number one in the world of stock car racing in 1999, an accomplishment that ushered him into the ranks of the NASCAR immortals.

point that you don't want to accept anything else. You realize that you're not going to be able to constantly, but there's no reason that we can't at least challenge and as long as we're challenging for wins and for the championship, then we'll be okay.

"It's not because my dad's got two or anything else, it's just that as long as I race now and having won a championship, that's what I want to continue to try and do."

DALE JARRETT'S CAREER STATS (THROUGH 1999)

YEARLY WINS AND POINTS TOTALS

YEAR	RACES	WINS	2-5	6-10	CHAMPIONSHIP POINTS POSITION
1984	3	0	0	0	n/a
1986	1	0	0	0	n/a
1987	24	0	0	2	n/a
1988	29	0	0	1	23
1989	29	0	2	3	24
1990	24	0	1	6	25
1991	29	1	2	5	17
1992	29	0	2	6	19
1993	30	1	11	5	9
1994	30	1	3	5	16
1995	31	1	8	5	13
1996	31	4	13	4	3
1997	32	7	13	3	2
1998	33	3	16	3	3
1999	34	4	20	5	1

VICTORIES IN NASCAR'S GREATEST SUPERSPEEDWAY EVENTS

Daytona International Speedway: Daytona 500
1993, 1996, 2000

Daytona International Speedway: Pepsi 400
1999

Charlotte Motor Speedway: Coca-Cola 600
1996

Indianapolis Motor Speedway: Brickyard 400
1996, 1999

Talladega Superspeedway: Winston 500
1998

PHOTOGRAPHY CREDITS

Allsport/ ©Jonathan Ferrey: pp. 63, 72-73, 85, 90;
©Craig Jones: p. 70; ©Robert Laberge: p. 86; ©Jamie
Squire: pp. 82-83, 92-93; ©David Taylor: Endpapers,
pp. 5, 44, 53, 54-55, 94

Associated Press/Wide World Photos: p. 80

©Tom Bernhardt: pp. 34, 36, 40, 45

International Speedway Corporation/ NASCAR
Archives: pp. 14, 16, 17, 22, 24, 25 top

©Frank Moriarty: pp. 42-43

©Mike Slade: pp. 20-21, 23, 25 bottom, 26, 27, 28, 29,
30-31, 32, 33

SportsChrome USA/ ©Greg Crisp: p. 6; ©Evan Pinkus:
pp. 51, 79; ©Brian Spurlock: pp. 2, 7, 10-11, 18-19, 50,
58, 59, 64, 65, 66-67, 68, 69, 71, 74, 76, 78, 81, 89

SportPics/ ©Scott Cunningham: pp. 38-39, 41

©Steve Swope Photography: pp. 8-9, 47, 48-49, 52,
56, 57, 60-61, 62

UPI/Corbis-Bettmann: pp. 12-13, 15

BIBLIOGRAPHY

Fielden, Greg. *Forty Years of Stock Car Racing*,
vol. 1–4. Surfside Beach, South Carolina:
Galfield Press, 1988, 1989, 1990.

———. *Forty Years of Stock Car Racing: Forty
Plus Four.* Surfside Beach, South Carolina:
Galfield Press, 1994.

———, and Peter Golenbock. *Stock Car Racing
Encyclopedia.* New York: Macmillan, 1997.

Moriarty, Frank. *Sunday Drivers: NASCAR
Winston Cup Stock Car Racing.*
Charlottesville, Virginia: Howell Press, 1994.

———. *The Encyclopedia of Stock Car Racing.*
New York: MetroBooks, 1998.

Various. *Goodwrench Service Racing Media Guide.*

Various. *NASCAR Winston Cup Series Media
Guide.* Winston-Salem, North Carolina:
Sports Marketing Enterprises, various years.

Various writers of *The Charlotte Observer. Dale
Earnhardt: Rear View Mirror.* Champaign,
Illinois: Sports Publishing Incorporated, 1998.

Vehorn, Frank. *The Intimidator*, 4th ed. Asheboro,
North Carolina: Down Home Press, 1999.

INDEX

"Alabama Gang," 32, 50
Allison, Bobby, 32, 50
Allison, Davey, 22, 26, 35, 37, 50, 84
Allison, Donnie, 32, 35
Atlanta Motor Speedway, 58, 69, 84–87

Baker, Buddy, 35
Bodine, Geoffrey, 46
Bonnett, Neil, 32, 34
Brickyard 400, 58, 65, 74
Bristol International Raceway, 35, 44, 58, 70–71, 80
Burton, Jeff, 70, 74–75, 77
Busch Grand National Series, 23, 24, 26, 27, 27, 28–29, 30–31, 32, 32, 33, 91

California Speedway, 72
Charlotte Motor Speedway, 33, 35, 38–39, 46, 52, 58
Chevrolet, 17, 25, 28
Chevrolet Lumina, 40, 42, 45
Childhood, 10, 22, 22–25

Darlington Raceway, 32–35, 70, 80
Dash Series, 24, 27
Daytona 500, 32, 35, 44, 45–46, 47, 56, 62, 65, 82–83, 86, 89, 92
Daytona International Speedway, 44, 54–55, 75–77
Donlavey, Junie, 6
Dover Downs International Speedway, 58, 80

Earnhardt, Dale, 28, 32, 45, 46, 56, 58, 65, 71–72, 75–77, 81, 91
Earnhardt, Dale, Jr., 91
Earnhardt, Ralph, 17
Elliott, Bill, 35, 65
Evernham, Ray, 91

Ford Motor Company, 17, 56
Ford Taurus, 7, 8–9, 53, 54–55, 57, 62, 65, 66–67, 80, 82–83, 86
Ford Thunderbird, 34, 35, 37, 50, 52
Foyt, A.J., 35
France, Bill, Sr., 17

Gant, Harry, 35
"Gentleman Ned." See Jarrett, Ned.
Gibbs, Joe, 37, 40–46, 44
Golf, 24–25, 88
Gordon, Jeff, 42–43, 45, 46, 58, 62, 75, 77, 91

Gordon, Robby, 6
Grand National Series championship, 16, 17, 19
Gurney, Dan, 35

Hamilton, Bobby, 74
Hickory Speedway, 14, 22, 25, 26, 27
Homestead-Miami Speedway, 63, 80, 81, 84

Indianapolis Motor Speedway, 57, 58, 65, 74, 78, 78
Irvan, Ernie, 35, 50, 52, 53, 56, 65, 84
Irwin, Kenny, 65, 68
Isenhower, Horace, 27

Jarrett, Glenn, 19
Jarrett, Kelley, 87
Jarrett, Ned, 6, 10, 14–19, 14–18, 22, 46, 65, 92
Jarrett, Patti, 19, 42
Joe Gibbs Racing, 40–46, 52
Johnson, Junior, 17, 35, 50
Jones, Parnelli, 35

Kenseth, Matt, 91
Kulwicki, Alan, 34, 35, 50

Labonte, Bobby, 75, 77, 80, 87
Labonte, Terry, 54–55, 58, 70
Las Vegas Motor Speedway, 69, 90
Late Model Sportsman Division, 27
Lentz, David, 14
Limited Sportsman Division, 25–27
Long, Bondy, 17
Lorenznen, Fred, 35
Lowe's Motor Speedway, 74, 80

Makar, Jimmy, 42, 45
Marcis, Dave, 54–55
Martin, Mark, 35, 37, 62, 69, 72, 76, 77, 80
Martinsville Speedway, 20–21, 28, 71, 80
Mayfield, Jeremy, 65
McReynolds, Larry, 52
Michigan International Speedway, 35–37, 58, 75
Miller, Don, 42
Moore, Bud, 6

New Hampshire International Speedway, 77
Newton-Conover High School, 24–25
North Carolina Speedway, 69, 81

Orange Speedway, 28

Palmer, Arnold, 88
Panch, Marvin, 17
Parrott, Buddy, 56
Parrott, Todd, 56, 58, 62, 65, 68, 71, 74, 75, 80, 87, 88, 91, 92
Pearson, David, 17, 35
Pearson, Larry, 22
Penske, Roger, 42
Petree, Andy, 25
Petty, Kyle, 22, 26, 34, 35
Petty, Richard, 17, 91
Phoenix International Raceway, 58, 81
Pocono International Raceway, 34, 35, 36, 53, 58, 75, 78
Pontiac, 28, 29, 30–31, 32
Pruett, Scott, 6

Quality Care Service/Ford Credit team, 58, 62, 65, 78, 80, 82–83, 91

Rahal, Bobby, 35
Ranier, Harry, 50
Richmond International Raceway, 42–43, 58, 72, 80
Roberts, Glenn "Fireball," 17
Robert Yates Racing, 46, 50–93
Rudd, Ricky, 85

Schrader, Ken, 62
Sears Point Raceway, 75
Southern 500, 19
Squier, Ken, 46
Stewart, Tony, 77, 80, 91
Stricklin, Hut, 52
Summerall, Pat, 6

Talladega Superspeedway, 58, 71–72, 81
Texas Motor Speedway, 70
Turner, Curtis, 35

Unser, Al, Jr., 56

Wallace, Kenny, 52, 77
Wallace, Rusty, 35, 42, 75
Watkins Glen International, 80
Wells, Cal, 6
Winston Cup Series, 28–29
   Joe Gibbs Racing, 40–46
   Robert Yates Racing, 50–93
   Wood Brothers, 32–37
Winston Cup Series championship, 80, 81, 81, 84–93
Wood Brothers, 32–35, 46

Yarborough, Cale, 6, 29, 32, 50
Yates, Robert, 50, 52, 56, 91

Zervakis, Emanuel "Manny," 28